Looking at...
FIGHTING
WARS

Ali Brownlie

WAYLAND

First published in 2009 by Wayland

Copyright © Wayland 2009

Wayland
338 Euston Road
London NW1 3BH

Wayland Australia
Level 17/207 Kent Street
Sydney NSW 2000

Produced for Wayland by
White-Thomson Publishing Ltd

+44 (0) 845 362 8240
www.wtpub.co.uk

Editors: Sonya Newland and Katie Powell
Designer: Robert Walster

British Library Cataloguing in Publication Data
Brownlie Bojang, Ali, 1949-
   Looking at wars
   1. War - Juvenile literature
   I. Title II. Wars
   355'.02

ISBN: 9780750259033

Picture Credits
AKG Photo, London: 20; Camera Press: 7 (Novosti), 8, 39 (Donald McCullin/ILN); Corbis: 9 (Goran Tomasevic), 23 (Jerry Lampen/Reuters), 35 (Benjamin Lowy), 41 (Khaled El-Fiqi/epa); Howard Davies, Exile Images: *contents* top, 21, 24, 30, 31, 32, 44, 45; Getty Images: 29 (AFP); The Illustrated London News Picture Library: 34; The John F. Kennedy Library: 40; Peter Newark's Military Pictures: 10; Popperfoto: *contents* bottom (Jason Reed, Reuters), 4, 5 (Nayef Hashlamoun, Reuters), 6, 11 (Corinne Dufka, Reuters), 12 (Jason Reed, Reuters), 15, 19, 22, 26, 27, 33 (Greg Bos, Reuters), 37 (Jayanta Shaw, Reuters), 38 (Laszlo Balogh, Reuters), 42, 43 (Ulli Michel, Reuters); Topham Picturepoint: 13, 14, 16, 17 (J. Gapps, Associated Press), 18 (Associated Press), 25 (Press Association), 28, 36 (D. Brauchli, Associated Press).

Printed in China

Wayland is a division of Hachette Children's Books, an Hachette UK company.
www.hachette.co.uk

CONTENTS

Wars and warring

Wars can be divided into two types. In an international war, the people of one country fight the people of another country. A civil war is when groups within the same country fight each other.

What is war?

It is not easy to say when a skirmish or fighting becomes a war. However, a war is usually 'declared' by a political leader who has power and authority. Both sides – as well as other countries – usually recognize that they are fighting a war.

⬇ Most modern armies have female members. These soldiers are taking part in a parade in China.

The problems of civil war

Many modern wars are civil wars and often involve criminal gangs. Civil wars are not officially declared. There are international laws that protect soldiers and people living in countries at war. However, if war is not officially declared it can be hard to enforce these laws. It can also be more difficult to end a civil war, as either side may not accept peace treaties.

Even though war makes some acts of violence legal, acts against civilians and very brutal acts, such as torture, are still considered crimes by law.

↑ Young people, such as this young Palestinian, are often involved in fighting because they are more easily influenced.

FACT

Millions of people around the world are members of the armed forces. China has the largest number of troops, with more than two million. North Korea has the highest number in relation to its population — 47 per 1,000.

INTERNATIONAL INSTITUTE FOR STRATEGIC STUDIES, *THE MILITARY BALANCE 2008.*

A brief history of war

People have been fighting wars for as long as history has been recorded. The earliest known wars were fought over food and land. People used clubs, spears and stones as weapons.

By the nineteenth century, wars were fought using more advanced weapons, such as rifles, machine guns and artillery. These wars occurred on a much larger scale. European countries, such as Britain and Germany, fought to own land all over the world and to establish empires.

⬇ During World War I, women took jobs in factories making weapons, as many men were away fighting.

Two world wars

By 1914, two powerful groups of countries had formed. These two groups fought each other in World War I. Soldiers fought hand-to-hand in the trenches. By the time World War II broke out in 1939, bombing from the air and long-range artillery kept armies further apart. However, there were more civilian casualties – people killed or injured – because of these attacks from a distance.

The Cold War

After World War II, two 'superpowers' emerged – the USA and the Soviet Union (USSR). They each developed weapons of mass destruction, such as nuclear weapons, although they never went to war. This period was known as the Cold War. In the 1990s, both countries agreed to reduce the amount of weapons they had. However, in 2007, Russian prime minister Vladimir Putin announced plans to build more nuclear weapons because he believed that the USA wanted to invade Russia.

⬆ The May Day parade in Red Square, Moscow, displayed the Soviet Union's military might.

FACT

In 1986, the global stockpile of nuclear weapons peaked at 69,490. Since then it has dropped dramatically. There are now thought to be fewer than 20,000 nuclear weapons around the world, and that number is still falling.

Why do wars start?

Wars happen in different places and for different reasons. Although many people suffer during wars, some people benefit from them. If a country's leader is successful during wartime, it can improve his or her popularity. Sometimes wars are started on purpose to make a political leader more popular.

⬇ The former British prime minister, Margaret Thatcher, speaks to naval officers who had been fighting in the Falklands War (1982).

Changing lives

Countries fight wars because they think if they are successsful they will be more important in the world. They may be able to trade with more countries, for example, or own more land.

People also fight wars to defend themselves, because they are afraid, or because they think their lives will improve if the war is won. Few people benefit from war, though.

Religion and beliefs

People from different religions or who have different beliefs have fought wars for hundreds of years. In the twentieth century, for example, the different beliefs of Capitalism and Communism led to the Korean and Vietnam wars. Religious differences have been a factor in many conflicts, including the civil war in Sudan, between Muslims in the north and Christians in the south.

⬆ Women, children and other civilians have increasingly become involved in the effects of wars. This is a street in Baquba, Iraq, in 2007.

Fighting wars

When war breaks out, young men often have no choice about whether or not to fight because of a law called conscription. In some countries, women also have to join the military in times of war. People can be sent to prison or even executed if they refuse to go to war in some countries.

⬇ This poster, protesting against the Vietnam War, is based on a World War I poster, which read 'I Want You for the US Army'.

Avoiding conscription

During the Vietnam War in the 1960s and 1970s, many American men refused to join the army because they thought that the war was wrong. Some were sent to prison, but others escaped to Canada, where they stayed until the war was over.

Escaping poverty

If people are poor, they may think that fighting will result in a better life, but this is rarely the case. Wars often occur when people think there are no peaceful ways to escape poverty.

Mercenary soldiers

Some people enjoy fighting. They may even enjoy killing others. Some of these people find it difficult to adjust to life once a war is over, so they become mercenaries – people who work as private soldiers for anyone who will pay them.

⬆ These troops from the Comoros Islands, near Madagascar in the Indian Ocean, are led by a mercenary soldier from France.

CASE STUDY ▸ CASE STUDY ▸ CASE STUDY ▸ CASE STUDY ▸

Pedro, a young man in El Salvador, was on his way home from visiting some friends when he was stopped at an army checkpoint. He was ordered off the bus and taken to the barracks, and there he was forced to join the army. He was trained for four months and was then sent to fight. He was told that if he did not fight, he would be killed. He was injured and spent three months in hospital, but he never understood who or why he was fighting.

Why do children fight in wars?

There are thought to be around 300,000 child soldiers all over the world. Some child soldiers are as young as six. Many of them are girls.

Modern infantry weapons are simple to operate and very light, so children can easily use them. Armies like to recruit children because they are easily persuaded to fight and they are often not afraid. This is probably because they do not realize what is happening. Some child soldiers have said that they only killed small children, because they believed this was less serious than killing adults.

⬇ This 12-year-old boy is part of a rebel army fighting against the military government that has ruled Burma for the past 20 years.

 Young schoolchildren parading in military uniforms in Angola during the civil war that ended in 2002.

Civil war in Sierra Leone

Around 20,000 children fought on both sides of the civil war in Sierra Leone between 1991 and 1999. Many were taken from their villages after they had been forced to watch their families being killed. Some children became soldiers because it was the only way to get food. Others fought to avenge the deaths of their families. After the war, special centres were set up where children could receive counselling and help to return to normal life.

'When I was killing, I felt like it wasn't me doing these things. I had to because the rebels threatened to kill me.'

PETER, 12, WHO HAD BEEN KIDNAPPED BY REBEL FORCES DURING SIERRA LEONE'S CIVIL WAR

War crimes

International law now says that making children under 15 fight is a war crime. Anyone who recruits child soldiers can be sent to prison. However, children are still forced to fight in wars in many countries.

War and new technology

Computers and information technology have created new systems that can guide missiles and bombs with great accuracy. These systems use satellites, computer maps and laser beams, and they can be controlled remotely to hit any target – a tank, military headquarters or an airfield. They can even hit a target the size of a door from thousands of kilometres away.

Problems with technology

Today, armed forces rely heavily on technology to direct weapons, and to send and receive information. This can cause problems if a computer system fails, though. There are also problems with hackers – people who break into computer systems and take control of them.

FACT

The USA is the world's biggest arms exporter, supplying around 40 per cent of the developing world's arms and ammunition.

STOCKHOLM INTERNATIONAL PEACE RESEARCH INSTITUTE.

← A US commander stands watch over computers at the North American Aerospace Defense Command.

Wars of the future

Many people believe that future wars will involve battles in cyberspace, with countries, terrorist groups and even individuals fighting across the Internet.

In 2005, the USA revealed that it had put together a team of experts called the Joint Functional Component Command for Network Warfare (JFCCNW). This group is there to defend US military systems and to find ways of attacking enemy computer systems.

⬆ These Patriot missiles in Saudi Arabia are designed to shoot down incoming enemy missiles in mid-air.

Types of war

Land is vital to people. They need it to grow food and as a source of water. Rivers often flow from one country into another and conflicts can be caused if the people in one country interfere with the water supply. For example, they may use up too much of the water, or cause it to be polluted before it reaches neighbouring countries.

Land ownership

People may believe a particular area is important, or belongs to them, because their ancestors lived there or because it has a religious significance. This is the case in the Middle East, where Jews and Arabs have fought for many years.

➡ Britain and Argentina both believed that they owned the Falkland Islands, and fought a war over them. Over 1,000 soldiers died in this war.

Trade wars

People also fight wars over land because of the precious resources it contains, such as oil or minerals. People may also fight over new technology or the trade in drugs such as heroin. These are called trade wars.

There have been several wars over oil in recent years. When Iraq invaded Kuwait in 1991, several Western countries, led by the USA, moved in to drive the Iraqis out. These countries helped Kuwait because it is one of the world's main oil-producing countries – and the West needed Kuwait's oil.

⬇ The deliberate burning of oil wells by the USA as the Iraqi troops retreated at the end of the Gulf War created enormous environmental problems.

Fighting for independence

In the first half of the twentieth century, many countries in Africa and Asia were still colonies of European powers. Between the 1940s and the 1960s, several of them gained their independence. Some won independence without going to war, but there were several harsh conflicts. Algeria fought for eight years to be free from French rule, for example.

Africa divided

Colonialism led to other kinds of wars, too. By the end of the nineteenth century, European powers had shared out the African continent without considering all the different ethnic groups that lived there. As a result, some groups were divided by the new boundaries, while others found themselves living next to old enemies.

⬆ French troops fight to control demands for independence from the Algerian people.

The Biafran War

The problems between ethnic groups in Africa worsened when African countries gained independence. In Nigeria, for example, the Igbo people in the south-east tried to become a separate state, and fighting broke out in July 1967. The new state, Biafra, was not equipped to fight a war, and more than one million people are thought to have died.

'Living in Biafra was like living in hell. We lived in bombed-out buildings, old schools or refugee camps. We stood in long lines to receive food flown into Biafra by charity organizations.'
GRACE ASIKA, A BIAFRAN REFUGEE

➔ A heavily armed soldier in 1967, during the Biafran War in Nigeria.

Exploiting fear

When people feel threatened, or if they are in a difficult situation, they may look for someone to blame for their problems. Ruthless leaders can exploit people like this and encourage them to pick on anyone who is different from them. They may target people who follow a different religion or who have a different background to them.

⬇ Anne Frank is one of the best-known victims of the Holocaust.

The Holocaust

Times were hard in Germany in the 1930s. People were poor, and they became anxious about the future. Hitler's Nazi government blamed the Jews, and this paved the way for the Holocaust in World War II, and the deaths of six million Jews.

CASE STUDY ▸ CASE STUDY ▸ CASE STUDY ▸ CASE STUDY ▸

Anne Frank and her family, who were Jewish, fled to the Netherlands during World War II and hid for nearly two years from the Nazis in an attic in Amsterdam. Anne kept a diary of her thoughts and fears about being caught and also about her everyday life. The family was eventually discovered and taken away by the Nazis. In 1945, Anne died in Belsen concentration camp, aged 14. Her diary was published after the war.

The Khmer Rouge

In the 1970s, Pol Pot was the ruler of Cambodia. He used an army called the Khmer Rouge to make people obey him. Anyone who was thought to be clever, even if they only wore glasses or could speak another language, might be killed. These massacres came to be known as the time of 'The Killing Fields'.

Wars like this are often the most shocking, because friends and neighbours end up fighting one another. Often people do not even understand why they are fighting.

FACT

Cambodia has the world's highest rate of orphans and widows as a result of the actions of Pol Pot's horrific regime in the 1970s.

⬇ These human skulls are part of a memorial to the people killed by the Khmer Rouge.

Rules of war

War crimes are acts carried out in wartime that target civilians, or use unnecessary violence, cruelty and torture against soldiers and prisoners of war. In the twentieth century, terrible crimes against humanity were carried out in the name of war, such as mass murder, genocide and ethnic cleansing.

⬇ William Calley, who was found guilty for his part in the My Lai massacre, leaving court in April 1971.

The My Lai massacre

In November 1969, during the Vietnam War, 567 unarmed Vietnamese peasants, mainly women and children, were killed in the village of My Lai by American soldiers.

When they were asked to explain their actions, the soldiers said that they were only obeying orders given by their superiors. Although one of the officers spent four years in prison for what happened, all charges were dropped against the others involved.

Ethnic cleansing in Serbia

Throughout the 1990s, Serbs carried out ethnic cleansing in the regions they controlled. All non-Serbs were driven out of this area. Under the leadership of Radovan Karadzic, Muslims were persecuted, and around 8,000 of them were killed. Karadzic was arrested for war crimes in 2008, and was tried by the International Tribunal in the Hague. His policy reminded many people of the Holocaust in the 1940s.

FACT

In 2007, world military expenditure was around US $1,339, an increase of six per cent over 2006.
The USA's military spending accounted for 45 per cent of the world total.

STOCKHOLM INTERNATIONAL PEACE RESEARCH INSTITUTE.

⬇ Radovan Karadzic is led into the International Criminal Tribunal to begin his trial for war crimes, in 2008.

War and international law

There have been rules about how people should act in wartime for thousands of years. The ancient Egyptians, Greeks and Romans had clear codes of conduct. The Bible, the Qur'an and other religious texts contain laws that say people should show respect for their enemies.

⬇ A Red Cross member takes care of a Rwandan refugee child in Zaire in 1997. More than 10 years later there are still 100,000 Rwandan refugees.

The Geneva Conventions

In 1859, a young Swiss banker, Henri Dunant, witnessed the terrible suffering of soldiers during a battle. He campaigned for better treatment of the wounded in warfare.

This led to the creation of the Geneva Conventions, which set out rules about how soldiers should be cared for, and how civilians and prisoners should be treated. The International Red Cross was set up to make sure that the Geneva Conventions were carried out.

Human rights

Since World War II, international law has tried to protect human rights. In 1948, the United Nations Universal Declaration of Human Rights was created, along with laws to prevent and punish people who carry out genocide.

The International Court of Justice was created in 1945 to resolve disputes between countries before conflict developed. However, the power of the court depends on countries agreeing to recognize its authority.

⬆ The Geneva Conventions state that prisoners of war should be well treated. These World War II prisoners at Colditz Castle in Germany are enjoying a game of volleyball.

The Nuremberg trials

The International Military Tribunal at Nuremberg was set up in 1945 to try the Nazis who had organized the holocaust of Jews, gypsies and homosexuals. This was the first time people were asked to account for their personal actions during war.

Hermann Goering, one of Hitler's right-hand men, committed suicide in prison just a few hours before he was due to be executed for his war crimes. Alleged World War II criminals are still being brought to trial today.

← Hermann Goering (facing the camera) talks to fellow accused Nazis at the Nuremberg war crimes trial in 1946.

International tribunals

After many wars, when war crimes are thought to have taken place, the United Nations holds an International Criminal Tribunal to name people who are believed to be responsible and to put them on trial. It often takes many years for everyone involved to be tried for their war crimes.

'I feel that justice should be done so that other people should not have similar experiences. Those who did these things should be punished for what they have done. We see people walking around who did things to us and we don't know if anything will be done to them.'

UWAMBEYI ESPERANCE, WHOSE HUSBAND AND BABY WERE KILLED IN RWANDA

← In 1998, General Pinochet was held in Britain for crimes he was believed to have committed in Chile in 1973. He was eventually allowed to return safely to Chile for health reasons.

The impact of war

Modern technology means that soldiers often do not need to fight each other face to face. Unfortunately, though, as weapons have become capable of striking at longer ranges, more civilians are being killed in times of war.

Civilian casualties

During World War I (1914–18), only five per cent of casualties were civilians. By the end of the twentieth century, this number had risen to over 80 per cent. Most were women and children. Today, more children than armed soldiers are killed or disabled by war.

⬇ Phan Thi Kim Phuc was nine years old when she was photographed running from an attack during the Vietnam War.

Soldiers at close range can tell the difference between enemy soldiers and civilians, but landmines and other weapons cannot. Landmines can lie hidden for years. Thousands of people have been killed or maimed by stepping on landmines.

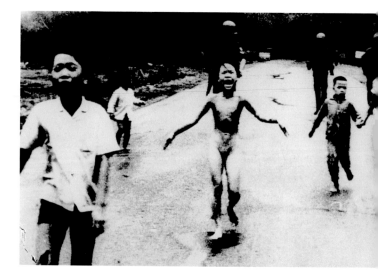

← Mohammad Fahim Rahimi lost his leg when he trod on a landmine in Afghanistan. He is now a professional powerlifter, and competed at the Paralympic Games in 2008.

There are people who believe that it is acceptable to target civilians during a war. Humanitarian trucks, hospitals, health clinics and aid stations have all been the targets of attacks.

Modern warfare

Chemical and biological weapons can spread poisons or disease over a wide area, killing or infecting everyone in their path. Although most countries have agreed never to use them, these weapons were used by Japan against China in 1942, and by Iraq against Kurdish rebels in the 1980s. On both occasions the victims were civilians who died in large numbers.

FACT

In the last 20 years, millions of children have died as a result of war and millions more have been disabled. Each month 2,000 men, women and children are killed, blinded or lose a limb because of landmines.

DEPARTMENT FOR INTERNATIONAL DEVELOPMENT.

Refugees

There are refugees all over the world, but most live in developing countries. These people have been forced to leave their homes because of war or conflict. Often they have had to leave in a hurry, taking only a few belongings. Many of them can never return to their homes. Other countries are not always happy to take in refugees, so they may end up moving around for a long time, trying to find a new home.

⬇ Children growing up in refugee camps in Gaza have spent their lives in close contact with violence.

Seeking safety

The largest group of refugees are five million Afghans, who left their country after the Soviet occupation between 1979 and 1989, and settled in Pakistan and Iran.

The largest group trying to find safety in Western countries are Iraqis. Many of them have also settled in the neighbouring countries of Syria and Jordan.

Helping refugees

The United Nations High Commission on Refugees (UNHCR) was created in 1951 to help refugees after World War II. Since then, the number of refugees has increased because of other conflicts. The UNHCR has won the Nobel Peace Prize for its work in helping refugees all over the world.

FACT

At the beginning of 2006, there were estimated to be 8.4 million refugees worldwide and around 34 million people who have been displaced by war and conflict – these are people who have been forced from their homes, but remain within the same country rather than settling overseas.

UNHCR, 2006.

← The UNHCR returns Tamil refugees to their homes in Sri Lanka in 1995.

CASE STUDY ▶ CASE STUDY ▶ CASE STUDY ▶ CASE STUDY ▶

Wali was born in Afghanistan and for the first few years of his life he went to school, played football and was happy like any other boy. But one night, men came to his house and took his father away and shot him. Fighting broke out in the city all around his family. They realized they would have to leave their home if they were to survive. Wali and his family now live in London.

After the war

The physical harm wars cause is plain to see. In countries such as Cambodia it is common to see children on crutches and young men in wheelchairs. But war can harm people in other ways, too.

Post-traumatic stress

Soldiers sometimes return from wars with a condition called post-traumatic stress disorder (PTSD). They may be bad-tempered, or have difficulty knowing where they are. They may feel depressed and have trouble getting on with their lives after the war. The effects of PTSD can be so bad that sufferers can no longer work.

⬆ Soldiers like these, injured by landmines in Sri Lanka, have to find new ways of earning a living.

CASE STUDY ▸ CASE STUDY ▸ CASE STUDY ▸ CASE STUDY ▸

Berta Ngheve, a 23-year-old Angolan, was walking with her sister near her home when she stepped on a mine. She heard a huge noise and then there was a terrible silence. A few seconds later she looked at her leg and realized that it was no longer there. Her daily chores – collecting water and firewood and preparing food – are more difficult to do. Berta now works as a tailor.

Famine

Poor countries often suffer famine in wartime. The war means that land cannot be farmed and food cannot be distributed properly. In the 2000s, Darfur in Sudan faced famine caused by the ongoing war in the country.

⬇ Remembering wars, and fellow soldiers that have been killed, is very important to many ex-soldiers.

Environmental damage

The environment suffers in other ways, too. During the Vietnam War, US troops used Agent Orange – a chemical that makes plants lose their leaves. This made it more difficult for the Vietnamese fighters to hide in the jungles. It also deprived civilians of food crops, and poisoned fish and water supplies. The land was left contaminated, and even today the Vietnamese people still have difficulty growing food crops.

Questions about war

People disagree about whether or not war can ever be justified. Pacifists argue that violence is never right. Others say that there are some situations where war is unavoidable.

Non-violent solutions

One of the best-known pacifists was Indian leader Mahatma Gandhi. He dedicated his life to winning independence for India, but he said that fighting was not the way to achieve this. He undertook a programme of 'satyagraha', which means non-violent resistance. People showed their resistance by resigning from their jobs and taking their children out of school, for example.

⬆ Mahatma Gandhi is still respected today for his belief that violence is not the way to solve the world's problems.

Imposing sanctions

Often sanctions are used as an alternative to fighting. This is when countries refuse to trade with other countries, so they may end up with shortages of food or medicines.

← Years of sanctions against Iraq have made the Iraqi people very poor. This woman lives on a rubbish dump, where she finds things to sell to earn money.

Justifying war

On the other hand, there are those who argue that fighting is justified if it reduces suffering and injustice. This argument was put forward by St Thomas Aquinas in the thirteenth century, and his ideas still influence the way in which most Western leaders justify military actions. People who believe that wars can be justified offer the fight against apartheid in South Africa as a good example of a justifiable war.

'Fight in the cause of Allah against those who fight you, but do not transgress limits.'
FROM THE QUR'AN, THE HOLY BOOK OF ISLAM
(in other words it is permitted to fight in self-defence)

Peacekeeping forces

After World War II, many people believed that a war like that should never happen again. The United Nations was formed in 1945 to promote world peace. One of its main aims was to prevent future wars by sending soldiers to troubled areas to try and prevent wars from breaking out.

UN soldiers come from the armies of all countries that are members of the United Nations. They wear light-blue berets or helmets and usually carry only light weapons. Their task is to keep peace between the warring sides. To send peacekeeping troops to an area, all members of the UN Security Council must agree that they should intervene in a dispute.

Relief work

Soldiers nowadays often play a major role in relief work when disasters strike. They use their skills and equipment to help the victims of floods, earthquakes and hurricanes. Aircraft from many different air forces help to drop food and medical supplies.

⬇ A British United Nations soldier watches for sniper fire while helping to carry the bags of a Bosnian Croat refugee as she is evacuated in 1993.

⬆ Indian soldiers help to search collapsed buildings for bodies after an earthquake in Bhuj in February 2001.

The war on drugs

Recently, the USA has started to send advisers, weapons and funds to support the Colombian army in its fight against drug producers. The US government provides training, helicopters, planes and bases in drug-producing areas.

FACT

In 2006, the USA provided 26 per cent of the money needed to send peacekeeping forces to troubled areas around the world, although it only accounted for 0.5 per cent of all UN peacekeeping troops.

UNITED NATIONS, 2006.

How do we know about wars?

Our televisions and newspapers are full of pictures and stories of war from many parts of the world. Journalists, TV crews and photographers keep the public informed about what is going on.

Journalists have traditionally acted as eye-witnesses and independent observers. They often risk their own lives to find information and take pictures. They believe it is their responsibility to report what they see as accurately as possible, without being influenced by what others think.

⬇ A Bosnian Serb officer tries to prevent a TV crew from filming at a United Nations-held airport in Sarajevo.

Public reactions

However, governments are not always happy for the public to know what really happens in wartime. During the Vietnam War, television coverage had the opposite effect from the one the US government wanted. People saw pictures of the horrors of modern warfare and they became angry about America's involvement.

⬆ Famous Vietnam War photographer Don McCullin's photos showed what war was like for civilians caught up in fighting and violence.

Hiding the truth

Propaganda is a powerful weapon in a war. Each side tries hard to make sure that the public are hearing what the authorities want them to hear. Governments have used cartoons, postcards, cinema advertising and even dropped leaflets from aeroplanes to get their message across.

'I do not believe we should stand neutrally between good and evil, right and wrong, aggressor and victim.'
MARTIN BELL, BBC REPORTER, CALLING ON THE BBC TO ABANDON NEUTRALITY IN REPORTING WAR

Intervention and mediation

There are around 6.7 billion people in the world. Weapons are more numerous and effective than ever before, and the threat of war is always present. Despite this, governments are trying harder than ever to keep peace between nations.

The Cuban Missile Crisis

In November 1962, many people feared that the USA and USSR would go to war over Soviet nuclear missiles based in Cuba, an island friendly to the Soviets that was very close to the American mainland.

FACT

In November 2001, President George W. Bush of the USA and Russian president Vladimir Putin signed the Strategic Offensive Reductions Treaty (SORT). This agreed to reduce nuclear weapons in the two countries to between 1,700 and 2,200 by the year 2012.

→ The US and Soviet leaders, John Kennedy and Nikita Khrushchev, at a meeting in Vienna in 1962. The two leaders avoided war when the Cuban Missile Crisis threatened world peace.

US president John Kennedy and Soviet premier Nikita Khrushchev negotiated over Kennedy's demand that the missiles must be removed. Both men were told by their military advisers to be prepared for nuclear war, but they came to an agreement in which they both compromised.

Mediation

In South Africa, Israel and Palestine, and Northern Ireland, a fragile peace has been maintained by keeping talks going and exploring all avenues for agreement. Often, a third country or organization such as the UN will chair the talks and act as a go-between for the opposing sides. This is called mediation.

⬇ UN Secretary General Ban Ki-mon, speaking at a press conference in 2008, during negotiations for peace between Israel and Palestine.

Long-term effects

The effects of war can carry on long after the fighting has ended. Any war, large or small, damages people and places. Much rebuilding needs to take place so that people can carry on with their lives.

Rebuilding lives

At the end of World War II, much of Europe was in ruins. Some people wanted to see Germany totally destroyed as a punishment for starting the war. But the countries that had won the war realized that Germany would have to be rebuilt, otherwise the German people would live in misery and poverty, which may eventually lead to another war.

⬇ After World War II, much rebuilding work took place in Germany to help revitalize the economy.

The USA spent billions of dollars helping European countries to rebuild after the war. This programme of aid was known as 'The Marshall Plan', after the US Secretary of State, George Marshall.

At the village of Neve Shalom Wahat al Salam in northern Israel, young Arab and Israelis study side by side. This is a country where conflict between the two peoples has been going on for over 50 years, and it is rare for Arabs and Israelis to mix. The village runs its own school and organizes courses for young Arab and Israeli students, where they come together to talk and share their lives with one another for a few days.

Reconciliation

In 1994, Nelson Mandela was elected president of South Africa. The previous leaders of South Africa had imprisoned him for 25 years for his opposition to apartheid. Mandela did not seek revenge, though. He felt that reconciliation could be brought about by openness, honesty and forgiveness. His government set up The Truth and Reconciliation Commission and promised a political pardon to all those prepared to testify and admit their part in maintaining the system of apartheid.

← Nelson Mandela salutes well-wishers as he leaves prison in 1990, after 25 years spent in captivity.

Resolving conflicts

Everyone faces conflict in their everyday lives. You might disagree about which television programme to watch or argue about which is the best sports team. These conflicts can be sorted out by negotiation and compromise, just like disagreements between countries.

Peaceful solutions

Just as governments may ask the UN to bring two sides together, young people may ask others for guidance or help in resolving a dispute. It is important for everyone to find peaceful solutions to disagreements, whether they are between individuals or whole nations.

⬇ A United Nations soldier from Ethiopia helps move refugees on the Rwanda-Zaire border in Africa in 1994.

Lessons from war

Many young people in schools across the world are learning about how to solve conflicts. Citizenship lessons are providing knowledge through examples, such as those we have looked at in this book. In many schools, young people are learning about conflict resolution through the experience of being involved in mediation schemes, where they help to resolve conflicts between other students.

⬆ In this puppet show, put on by the United Nations Children's Fund (UNICEF) in Burundi, the puppets are being used to show children how they can work through their differences.

CASE STUDY ▸ CASE STUDY ▸ CASE STUDY ▸ CASE STUDY ▸

Claire Gerrens is a pupil at Tanfield School in Durham. She volunteered for the school's mediation scheme. After a training course, Claire joined the team of young people who mediate between fellow pupils unable to resolve conflicts. They sit with the two people and encourage them to listen and talk to each other. 'It really works,' says Claire. 'I've seen people who couldn't talk without fighting really try hard to be friends. It helps to make all of us more confident about solving problems like this.'

GLOSSARY

Apartheid

The system in South Africa that separated people because of their race and colour.

Artillery

Heavy guns that fire large shells long distances.

Capitalism

An economic system based on the private ownership of wealth or capital.

Civilians

People who are not members of the military services.

Civil war

A war fought between two or more groups of people living in the same country.

Colonies

Territorial possessions owned by a ruling nation or state.

Communism

A political system that favours a classless society and the common ownership of property.

Conscription

Compulsory military service.

Ethnic cleansing

The attempt to remove from a region, either through expulsion or murder, anyone who is of a different ethnic group.

Ethnic group

A group of people who share the same origins and lifestyle.

Executed

To be killed as a punishment for a crime.

Famine

A severe shortage of food, which can cause the people in the affected area to suffer from hunger or starvation.

Genocide

The crime of destroying a national, ethnic, racial or religious group by mass murder.

Holocaust

An act of great destruction and loss of life. The term 'The Holocaust' refers to the attempt by Nazi Germany to systematically exterminate European Jews.

Humanitarian

Someone devoted to the promotion of human welfare.

Landmine

An explosive device buried in the ground designed to explode when a person steps on it.

Mercenaries

People hired to fight for a country other than their own.

Munitions

Weapons and military supplies.

Negotiations

Meetings where people or groups talk over their differences and try to reach an agreement that suits everyone.

Nobel Peace Prize

An award given every year to people or organizations who have advanced the cause of world peace.

Pacifist

Someone who is opposed to violence in any form and for any reason.

Propaganda

Information that is spread deliberately to promote a certain idea. Propaganda is often exaggerated or misleading.

Reconciliation

The process of bringing together, peacefully, people who were once enemies or opponents.

Refugee

Someone who has to flee to another country, often because of conflict and persecution in their own land.

Sanctions

A way of forcing a country to do something by encouraging other countries not to trade with them.

Skirmish

A minor short-term fight.

Torture

The deliberate infliction of pain and suffering on a person.

Tribunal

A form of judicial court.

FURTHER INFORMATION

ORGANIZATIONS

UK
The Anne Frank Trust UK
Star House
104-108 Grafton Road
London NW5 4BA
Tel: 020 7284 5858
www.annefrank.org.uk

British Red Cross
44 Moorfields
London EC2Y 9AL
Tel: 0844 871 11 11
www.redcross.org.uk

Centre for Conflict Resolution
Department of Peace Studies
University of Bradford
West Yorkshire BD7 1DP
Tel: 01274 235 235
www.brad.ac.uk/acad/confres/

The Refugee Council
240-250 Ferndale Road
Brixton
London SW9 8BB
Tel: 020 7346 6700
www.refugeecouncil.org.uk

USA
Peace Action
1100 Wayne Ave Suite 1020
Silver Spring, MD 20910
Tel: 301 565 4050
www.peace-action.org

UNICEF
3 United Nations Plaza
New York 10017
Tel: 212 326 7000
www.unicef.org

US Committee for Refugees
and Immigrants
2231 Crystal Drive, Suite 350
Arlington, VA 22202-3711
Tel: 703 310 1130
www.refugees.org

EUROPE
The International Federation
of Red Cross and Red Crescent
Societies
PO Box 372
CH-1211 Geneva 19
Switzerland
Tel: 22 730 42 22
www.ifrc.org

The Stockholm International
Peace Research Institute
Signalistgatan 9
SE-169 70 Solna
Sweden
Tel: 8655 97 00
www.sipri.org

FURTHER READING

Documenting History:
World War I
by Philip Steele
(Wayland, 2009)

Documenting World War II
series by various authors
(Wayland, 2007)

Ethical Debates: Terrorism
by David Smith
(Wayland, 2007)

Global Issues: Refugees
by Cath Senker
(Wayland, 2008)

INDEX